What Did They Wear?

A Look at What Soldiers Wore During the Revolutionary War

With Practical Advice on How You Can Put Together a Historically Accurate Impression

More Than 100 Photographs of Reenactors
Plus, More Than 60 Historical Images

Larry A. Maxwell

A Concise Guide
To Help Celebrate the 250th Anniversary
of the Revolutionary War

Larry A. Maxwell

What Did They Wear?

Cover Design by Matthew Maxwell

Reenactor photographs by Al Pochek
All Used By Permission
Individuals in the photographs are not identified by name as the pictures were taken at public events and were the property of Al Pochek.
Some photographs by Larry A. Maxwell. Others are credited if used.

Published by
Living History Productions
599 Route 311 Patterson, New York 12563
1130 Perry Rd., Afton, New York 13730
845-241-0035
LivingHistory.US

ISBN: 978-1-949277-16-6

COPYRIGHT 2025 – LARRY A. MAXWEL – All Rights Reserved
Photographs by Al Pochek – Used By Permission – All Rights Reserved

Larry A. Maxwell

Dedicated to The Memory of Al Pochek (1946-2024)
Great Photographer & Friend to the Reenacting Community

and to
**A Great Group of Friends Who Celebrated
the 225th Anniversary of Sybil Ludington's Ride in 2002**

George Warnacke*, Larry Maxwell, Nick Fenelli*, John "Jack" Klix*, Fred Lambert* (Hidden Behind Jack), Phil Weaver, and George Bock
* *Indicates Good Men Who Have Since Departed*

Table of Contents

Section	Page
Introduction	7
Four Levels of Appearance	11
Who Do You Want to Portray?	14
Types of Soldiers During the Revolutionary War	20
General Appearance	33
Small Clothes The Foundational Garments	36
Footwear	39
Headwear	40
Outerwear	44
Musicians	47
Military Accoutrements	48
How to Acquire The Necessary Items	52
Making Your Own Items	54
Practical Pointers for Making Some Items	58
Sutlers	66
Historical Images	73
The Royal Warrant of 1768	94
Helpful Books & Resources	99
About the Author	101

Larry A. Maxwell

Introduction

This is a concise guide to help those who would like to put together a historically accurate looking outfit to wear to a Revolutionary War event, or for a Sons of the American Revolution function, or for those who want to be a reenactor. Some today refer to reenacting as LARPing, which means Live Action Role Play.

This book uses modern photographs of reenactors who seek to portray people from the Revolutionary War as historically accurate as they can.

There are challenges when trying to put together a historically accurate looking outfit. It would be helpful if we had photographic evidence of what people wore during the Revolutionary War, but the first camera producing photographic images was not invented until more than forty years later. That means there are no photographs of people during the Revolutionary War.

The only sources we can use to determine a historically accurate look are paintings, sketches, journals, official written records, pension files, and newspaper accounts.

There are some problems with those sources. For example, paintings are a very commonly used resource for determining what people wore. Paintings done during the Revolution can be valuable to determine what people wore, but many artists used artistic license, and their works may not be completely reliable. Many artistic works, showing what people wore during the Revolution, were done after the war.

Many think newspaper accounts are dependable. I was an award-winning newspaper reporter and can guarantee all newspaper reports are biased and record what the writer chose to report and often exclude some details. Many newspaper accounts claim to be based on reports from eyewitnesses, but they give their own interpretation, which may not be correct.

Official records, like orders for clothing and supplies, are a very reliable source. The problem is what they ordered was not always acquired. For example, the New York Provincial Assembly ordered very specific-colored wools to differentiate its four Continental Line regiments in 1775. When the Bicentennial of the American Revolution approached many people began to attempt to reenact those regiments. For many years, reenactors outfitted their regiments based on those original orders. Researchers later discovered New York could not secure those colors of wool and got different ones instead.

Many have ancestors who served in a Local Militia so many like to portray the Militia during the Revolution. That is easier than portraying a Regular Soldier. Every colony had its own Militia. In some parts of Massachusetts, the Militia were often called Minutemen. A few other colonies also used that term. Those serving in most state militias were responsible for providing their own clothing and accoutrements. Some affluent towns issued uniforms for their militia. Most wore what they had. It was possible for older men to wear older style clothing they had on hand, such as longer frock coats or waistcoats, or French-fly breeches, which went out of fashion a few years before the Revolution.

Many people look at movies and television shows, with historical themes, especially documentaries, to determine what the people wore. Here is an important warning, many shows, even documentaries, are put together to make money for the producers. Having worked on numerous projects I can assure you those shows are usually not a good source for determining a historically accurate look. Most producers are more concerned with the story and not historical authenticity. Producers often ask me to provide them with generic Red Coats (meaning Regular Crown Forces) or generic Blue Coats (meaning Continental soldiers). Most of them have no idea there were more than eighty different uniforms used in different places at different times.

I worked with numerous people on film projects who told producers they were experts and as a result were hired to work on those projects about the Revolution. Yet, they were not experts and had little understanding about what people wore or used during that time.

I worked on one extensive multi-episode project for two years where the main costumer, armorer, and wrangler were all people who specialized in the War Between the States. They were nice people but had little or no knowledge of what was correct for the Revolutionary War, yet they told the producers they had that knowledge so they could get the job. As we worked together, they did not tell the producers about their lack of knowledge but constantly asked me to help them.

There was a popular television series about the Revolution, called *Turn*. The actors did a great job with what they were provided. The sad thing is the wardrobe left a lot to be desired. The women's clothing usually looked particularly good, but the men's clothing was often inaccurate. One of the key characters wore a leather steam punk jacket.

Going to a reenactment can be a better way to get an idea of what people wore.

Some reenactors do a lot of research and apply that to their impression. One problem for those looking for historical authenticity is many reenact for fun and try to look good but are not as concerned about historical authenticity, Some overlook important details. It is likely you will see various stages of authenticity at Revolutionary War reenactments.

You will probably see some inaccuracies: such as facial hair on men (totally appropriate for the War Between the States, but extremely uncommon during the Revolution), people wearing eyewear in the field (glasses were expensive, not very common, and mainly worn for reading back then), and you will probably see some well-meaning women portraying men at arms (only a few did that historically).

To get a historically accurate look takes research. Much of that research has already been done by historians and some reenactors. Some is compiled in various books mentioned at the end of this project. Much research is still ongoing.

Four Levels of Appearance
For Portraying
the Revolutionary War

1. Costume Party/School Play Look

If you are going to a costume party or to a gathering, where your goal is not historical accuracy, and just to get into the spirit and have a good time, most people are happy having what I call a Costume Party/School Play Look. You may be able to put something together with  things you already have, or you can buy a simple or elaborate costume online.

Here is a simple, no or low-cost way to make a Revolutionary War look. Wear a long-sleeved white shirt. Wear solid-colored pants tucked into long solid-colored socks. Wear a white or solid color silk scarf around your neck. Wear a solid-colored vest. Take a Cowboy Hat and push out the crown and cock up one side for the floppy hat look, or cock up three sides for the cocked hat look. You could also take a solid wool colored blanket, fold it into a triangle, drape it over your shoulders and secure it with a big cloak pin.

 Many well-meaning people buy a pattern and material from a fabric shop and make an outfit. Most of those patterns are inaccurate and the materials they recommend are often incorrect (only specific linen, wool, silk, and cotton were used). I STRONGLY recommend you DO NOT DO THIS. For a little more money, you can make, or buy, an outfit which is more historically accurate.

Here is a small but important point for a better look, Revolutionary War clothing most often fit very snuggly.

For those who want to make a more historically accurate impression, which is also appropriate for many living history events, The Living History Guild identifies three levels of reenacting looks as follows:

2. Apprentice

For the Apprentice Look, you must look historically accurate from 10 feet away. The Apprentice Look is for the beginner or casual reenactor. That is how I started as a reenactor. Our unit and some others gladly welcome people at this level.

The first thing you need to do for this impression is avoid ALL anachronisms. That means do not wear a wristwatch or ANY item which is out of place for this time period such as modern eyewear.

Many people who do this look buy or borrow items, some make them. If you make them you must understand all clothing during the Revolution was hand sewn. Some hand sewing back then looks a lot like machine sewing. Most of your clothing for an Apprentice look will probably be sewn on a machine

If you make items, there is a section on that in this book. Please use historically accurate patterns, such as some by J.P. Ryan. Avoid incorrect materials.

Jas. Townsend is a supplier who caters to the Apprentice look. You can modify some of their items for a better look.

For all looks, you should not have ANY facial hair. Even Mountain men and Pirates did not have facial hair during this period. The ONLY exception is if you are portraying a Hessian or some French who had mustaches, but no beards. My brother and many others I know usually have facial hair but shave before an event, so they look more accurate.

If you normally wear glasses and want a more historically accurate look, you should replace them for reenacting with contact lens. If you need corrective eyewear it should only be for reading. Some buy the inexpensive colonial glasses from Townsend and have prescriptions lens installed. I know some who forgo wearing corrective eyewear and just follow the blur in front of them.

Based on my observation, the Apprentice look accounts for about 60 percent of all reenactors. I am pleased to see many members of the Sons of the Revolution move from the Costume Look to the Apprentice Look. Some of them have even moved to the Journeyman Look, which is the next level.

3. Journeyman

The Journeyman is usually more dedicated than the Apprentice. Everything they wear, or use, is made with historically correct materials and according to historically accurate patterns. Everything looks good while standing next to them.

The seams which do not show can be done on a sewing machine.

From my observation, the Journeyman accounts for about 30 percent of reenactors.

4. Craftsman

The Craftsman is a very dedicated person. All patterns and fabrics they use are historically accurate. As there were no sewing machines back then all the clothing they wear is completely handsewn, even the seams you cannot see. The same is true of all accoutrements used which were also handmade.

Based on my observation, this accounts for about 10 percent of reenactors.

,

Larry A. Maxwell

Who Do You Want to Portray?

There are many different individuals or types of people from the Revolutionary War you could portray. You must determine specifically who, or what type of person, you want to portray.

1.   Ancestor

Numerous ancestors of mine served in the Revolutionary War. When I started re-enacting I chose to portray one of those ancestors, John Fancher of the 4th New York Regiment. Like many others, I thought that was what reenactors did.

If you want to portray one of your ancestors, determine what they did during the Revolution. Then determine what they wore. Were they a civilian who helped support the cause? Were they a member of the Continental Congress or a Colonial Assembly? Were they a blacksmith, innkeeper, or tradesman? There are different types of clothing for soldiers and for civilians depending on their occupation or role they played.

If your ancestor was a soldier or sailor, what type were they? Were they Militia or a Continental Soldier? Were they a Loyalist or a Regular British Soldier? Try to determine what regiment or unit they belonged to, also when and where they served. That will help you determine what they wore. Some of the soldiers served in more than one unit during the war so they could have multiple looks.

Many reenactors DO NOT have ancestors who served in the Revolution.

2.   Specific Historical Character

Some people want to portray a specific local or national historical figure. This could be a good idea for a local site or special commemorative events.

Two of the most popular portrayals people like to do are General George Washington or Benjamin Franklin. Some do them well, most do not. There is a

lot of documentation for those two. Many people in the public will not care how good you look when you do this, but I think you should do a good job no matter what you do.

If you are older and make a somewhat accurate impression of any Revolutionary War figure you will be surprised how many people will come up to you and call you General Washington. I never try to portray him, but it happens to me a lot. I personally recommend avoiding those portrayals unless you can do an exceptionally good job or if a commemoration needs one of these and none are available.

When I was working on a specific film project as an advisor and costumer, they hired someone who professionally portrayed George Washington. He bore a striking resemblance to Washington and could even mimic his handwriting. Prior to that he made many appearances doing that impression, but his uniform was a very gawdy inaccurate costume. I helped change his appearance to be more historically accurate.

I know a few, like John Koopeman III, who portray Washington very well.

Portraying a local historical figure with connections to the Revolution can be a good idea, especially if they are connected to a local site or local historic commemoration. That can help honor them. You should seek to do as accurate a portray as you can.

Keep in mind, most people had more than one outfit for different occasions.

3. Generic Historical Character

The Revolutionary War included many people other than soldiers who contributed to the cause. Most choose to portray a generic historical character rather than a specific individual.

You could portray a farmer, blacksmith, merchant, clergy, innkeeper, or any type of craftsman or tradesperson. It adds so much to living history if you demonstrate both what they wore and what they did.

3. General Soldier

Many people ask reenactors who they are portraying, assuming reenactors portray a specific individual. Few reenactors portray a specific named individual. Most portray a general soldier from a specific unit who served during a specific time, in a specific place during the war. That helps narrow down what they wore.

4. Militia Look is a Good Starting Look

A Militia look is a good place to start because most Militia wore civilian clothing, and everyone back then wore civilian clothing at some time. Most states had Militia Laws which required every able-bodied male to belong to the Militia.

All members of the Continental Congress, Committees of Safety, and Provincial Assemblies wore civilian clothing.

If you think at some point you might want to do Militia and maybe later a Continental soldier look, or even a Crown Forces soldier, I recommend you get white small clothes (explained later in this book). That can provide you with the opportunity to change your impression just by changing your coat.

5. Specific Reenacting Unit

If you want to join a specific reenacting group it is best to speak with them before you put together a look. Do not join a unit just because they are close to you or because you saw them at a reenactment. Do some research before joining. You must understand many reenacting groups have nice members and are fun to be with but may not be dedicated to being as historically accurate as possible, even though they may say they are. That may or may not be important to you.

What Did They Wear?

On the other hand, some units may be dedicated to historical authenticity but may not be pleasant to be with.

I recommend you consider a unit which is part of one of the Big Three National Organizations. Those help provide a unit with a level of accountability.

The national organizations of Revolutionary War reenactors are **The Brigade of the American Revolution**, **The British Brigade**, and **The Continental Line**. Each require applicant units to adhere to certain safety standards. Each organization has some outstanding historically accurate member units.

If you like serious historical authenticity you may want to consider joining a reenacting unit which belongs to The **Brigade of the American Revolution (BAR)**. It portrays both soldiers and civilians of the American Revolution from both sides. Member units must submit meticulous research documenting what they wear and use. Its events focus mainly on educating the public. It is the smallest of the three national organizations, so its events are generally small.

Some units like authenticity, but also like bigger events and recreating larger scale battle scenarios, so they join one of the other larger organizations. Some belong to both the **BAR** and one of the other larger organizations. The **BAR** will often do events along with The **Continental Line** and The **British Brigade**. My unit belongs to all three.

The **Continental Line** is a large organization comprised of units which portray the Continental Side and its allies during the Revolutionary War. Units portray specific regiments. Some portray units at specific times in the Revolution. They can portray Militia or Continental Line units. Many have female camp followers. Some have musicians and craftsmen. Some allow women to portray male soldiers, some do not.

The **Continental Lines** seeks to have its units look period correct, but its highest priority is safety as it focuses on portraying historical battle scenarios. Many of those scenarios are often large scale, something the **BAR** cannot do by itself.

Many **Continental Line** member units look very accurate historically. Once a unit is approved they are encouraged to follow historical appearance guidelines, but that is left up to individual units to monitor. Some units work hard to look historically accurate, but some are satisfied and welcome to stay at the Apprentice Level, as long as they are safe.

Most of The **Continental Line** units are good people to field with. Some units are particularly good interacting with the public. Some are more into doing battle scenarios than others. Many are like an enjoyable social club.

The **British Brigade** is a large organization which portrays the Crown Forces during the Revolution. That includes both Regular Crown Forces, Loyalists, as well as Tribal, and Hessian Forces.

The **British Brigade** focuses on both historical accuracy and safety. Applicant units must not only prove to be safe but must pass a rigorous authenticity inspection.

They often do large scale historical reenactments with the **Continental Line** and sometimes along with the **BAR**.

There are some historical inaccuracies allowed among the Big Three Organizations. Though discouraged by all three, facial hair is allowed in both the **BAR** and **Continental Line** but not in the British Brigade. All three organizations discourage the use of corrective eyewear, but all three allow it.

Historically, women were not allowed as a soldier in any army during the Revolution. A few women did disguise themselves as men and served. There were a few women, dressed as women, who did participate in some battles on the Continental side. One became known as Molly Pitcher.

As this book is being written only the **BAR** forbids women portraying men in the ranks, though some of their units do have women portraying men as musicians.

Though a unit may belong to one, or more, of the Big Three Organizations, some will be a better fit for you than others.

6.   Civilians & Families

Many reenacting units allow, and many encourage people to join who portray civilians or families during the Revolutionary War.

For most men portraying civilians, the Militia look will work.

Many women and children like to be part of keeping history alive.

Most reenacting units, like ours, gladly welcome people to portray women and children in the Revolution.

The **Brigade of the American Revolution** published a Woman's Clothing Guide which is one of the BEST resources to help put together a period correct impression for women.

Larry A. Maxwell

Types of Soldiers During the Revolutionary War

If you want to portray a soldier during the Revolutionary War you must determine what type of soldier you want to portray, You should determine what specific regiment they were with, as well as when and where they served. Some uniforms for some regiments changed during the war.

This is not meant to be a definitive work on all the different types of soldiers but addresses some of the most common ones.

The Continentals

The term Continentals refers to those who fought to oppose the Crown. That includes both the Continental Army and the Militia. The Crown usually referred to them as the *Rebels*. Sometimes they were referred to as *Americans* or as *Colonists* but that is not a truly clear description because technically everyone who lived in America and served on either side were Americans and Colonists.

The term *Patriot* means someone who is loyal to their country, During the early years of the war it was used to refer to people loyal to their country England. Gen. Howe of the British Army wrote that he lamented the fact George Washington was not a Patriot. Later in the war, and especially after the war, the term *Patriot* was applied to those who were loyal to the new United States and helped the cause during the Revolution.

It is important to understand the Continental Side had valuable assistance from people who came from other countries to help during the Revolution. They also ended up with official alliances with Spain and France who both sent troops.

1. Militia

Before the Revolution, all thirteen colonies had Local Militia Laws which required all able-bodied men, from at least 15 years of age and upwards, to belong to the militia. The Local Militia trained regularly following a specific military drill manual. They were there to help defend their town from any enemy which may arise. Each Militia was run by its own locality and then answered to the Colony. Unlike the Continental Army, most Militia or local community leaders selected their own leaders.

Most Militia members had to provide their own clothing. There was usually no uniformity in the look of their clothing. Some Militia in affluent areas, like around Boston, and in parts of Connecticut, issued uniforms to their members.

Some Militia Laws listed specific items each member of the Militia was to carry.

On April 19, 1775, there was no Continental Army. It was the members of the Lexington Militia who encountered the expeditionary force of Regular Soldiers sent to arrest the leaders of the Sons of Liberty. Then Militia from the surrounding areas responded to the alarm.

As word of Lexington and Concord spread throughout the Colonies it was local Milita from throughout New England who came to help.

2. The Continental Army

The Continental Army was formed on June 14, 1775, by the Continental Congress. That became the birthday of the United States Army and was considered a declaration of war by the Crown, though not by the Continental Congress.

Each colony was called upon to form regiments to serve in the Continental Army. The Colonial Assemblies selected officers. Each regiment answered to George Washington who was selected as General of the Continental Army. Officers officially had to be approved by the Continental Congress. That created some problems for Gen. Washington as some officers like Gen. Thomas Gage tried to circumvent Washington by finding allies in the Continental Congress.

Officers were personally responsible for the expenses of their regiment and had to request reimbursement from the Continental Congress. That meant a person had to be affluent, rather than experienced or qualified to be an officer. That caused serious problems and disenfranchised some outstanding officers like Benedict Arnold who complained he was not properly reimbursed.

Most soldiers in the Continental Army were issued some uniform items. Most regiments had one color for the body of their coat and another for the facings.

During the first year of the war, in 1775, New York regiments only received regimental coats. They had to provide their own small clothes and hats.

The regimental coats worn by the Continental Army looked similar to those worn by the Crown Forces. Some had plain buttons. Some had numbers on their buttons, some had letters to indicate their state. One exception was most Continental regiments did not have lace or tape around the buttons.

Like the Crown Forces, the regimental coats had non-functioning buttons. They were worn closed by means of two or three sets of hooks and hoops.

Some colonies had different uniforms for different areas. In 1775, during the first year of the war, New York had four different regimental coats, which were issued by region. By 1778, most of those regiments were issued different colored regimental coats.

In 1780, General Washington ordered all troops to wear blue regimental coats with different colored facings depending on which state they were from. Those regimental coats had buttons with USA on them. All states did not receive those.

The design of many coats changed as the war progressed. At the beginning of the war, some regiments wore regimental coats which extended down to just above the knee. Soon they became a little shorter. Later, some were made noticeably short and were often referred to as *short coats*.

Most coats, especially early in the war, not only had non-working buttons but also did not have pockets, only pocket flaps. Some had pockets in the linings.

In 1778, the French began to supply the Continental Army with both Blue Coats faced Red and Brown Coats faced Red. A lottery was held to determine what regiment got which color coat. Hence, they were sometimes called *Lottery Coats*. Some regiments never received the *Lottery Coats*.

In 1780, General Washington ordered the whole army to wear blue coats and assigned different facing colors to different regions. Many regiments followed those orders, some did not. Supplying the coats was a major problem.

The Continental Army was comprised of Infantry Regiments, as well as Artillery and mounted troops called Dragoons. Each regiment had its own Musicians.

Most Continental Artillery wore blue coats with red facings and yellow/gold lace around plain brass buttons, as well as yellow/gold trimmed cocked hats, like the Royal Artillery. There were some exceptions like Lamb's Artillery.

3. Levies

As the war progressed, Colonies were called upon to send some of their better soldiers from their Militia to serve alongside the Continentals. Those soldiers were called Levies. Levies wore their own regular Militia clothing.

4. Tribal Members

Members of various tribes served on both sides during the Revolutionary War. Very few do this impression.

If you have tribal ancestry you may want to do a portrayal of a member of your ancestor's tribe. If you do not have such ancestry it is not looked upon favorably by some tribes for you to make such an impression.

5. Naval Forces

The Continentals used boats as part of their effort as early as April 1775, when two sailors rowed Paul Revere across from Boston to Charleston. Often the sailors were members of the militia.

On October 13, 1775, the Continental Congress established the United States Navy. Most seamen wore baggy breeches called sloops and a different style coat.

6. Allies of the Continentals

Throughout the Revolution some individuals from other countries offered their services to the Revolution. Some of the memorable ones were the Marquis de Layfette from France, Thaddeus Kosciuszko and Vladimir Pulaski, from Poland, and Baron Von Steuben, from Prussia.

From early in the war leaders of the Continental Congress, such as John Adams and Benjamin Franklin sought allies for the Revolution.

O The Spanish

The Spanish were one of the Continental Army's first committed allies.

Spain allowed the Continentals use of their ports in Puerto Rico.

The Spanish Governor of Louisiana, Bernardo de Galvez and his Spanish troops provided invaluable aide to the Continentals. They secured the Mississippi. In 1779, they attacked and defeated the Crown Forces and drove them from Florida. Some descendants of those men later settled in Central and South America.

O The French

The French, who were enemies of England at the time of the Revolution, helped the Continentals by first sending older muskets and regimental coats.

In 1778, the French officially joined the war. They came to America with their Infantry, Cavalry, and Navy.

What Did They Wear?

Photo By Angelina M. Vorno

Many French Troops wore white regimental coats with various facings. Some wore blue coats. Their lapel facings were generally shorter than the Continentals and Crown Forces.

In honor of the French Alliance, in 1778, Col. Henry Livingston secured white regimental coats, faced red for his 4th New York Regiment.

The uniform also included a unique wool felt hat with a black horsehair crest, similar to what dragoons wore.

The Alliance Cockade

In honor of the French alliance, starting in 1778, many of the Continentals added a piece of white linen or silk to their cocades.

Larry A. Maxwell

The Crown Forces

The Crown Forces were comprised of British Regular Soldiers, the Royal Navy, Royal Artillery, Engineers, Loyalists, and German Troops.

1. British Regular Army

The British Regular Army was a professional Army. Being in the Regular Army was an occupation. The minimum age for a soldier was 15. Its officers were landed gentry. That meant they owned land, unlike the general population. An enlisted man, who was not landed gentry could never become an officer.

One of the main roles of the Regular Army in America was to maintain peace and order. Later they were used to try to end the rebellion.

The Regular Army was comprised of various regiments. All Infantry regiments wore red regimental coats. That earned them, the nickname in America, *Redcoats* or *Lobster Backs*.

Each Regiment was distinguished by the facing color and their own regimental lace around the buttons. Most regiments had their own distinctive buttons.

Soldiers for the Regular Army were recruited from various regions throughout the United Kingdom. Some regiments were comprised mainly of Irish or Welsh. Some regiments were comprised mainly of Scottish Highlanders who had their own distinctive uniforms. That included the great kilt, sporrans, kirks, dirks, and basket hilt swords.

In 1746, Parliament passed the Dress Act which outlawed the wearing of any clan clothing, including a kilt or clan tartan. An exception was granted to the Scottish Highlanders in the army who were loyal to the Crown. Many Scotlanders opposed to English rule derogatorily called those people, *The Black Watch*. Those who were called that took it as a badge of honor.

The 71st Regiment of Foot became known as *The Black Watch*.

The Regular British Army was comprised of regiments with ten companies. Each company had its own company number. For example, one Company within the Tenth Regiment was called The Tenth Regiment Company One.

Each regiment usually had eight Hat Companies, one Light Infantry Company, and one Grenadier Company.

O **Hat Company**

Most soldiers in the Regular Army were in Hat Companies. Those in the Hat Companies were what people usually picture as Regular Soldiers.

These usually wore cocked hats with a cockade and a button with their regimental number.

Some companies had the buttons on their regimental coats spaced or grouped to distinguish them from other companies. For example, the Second Company often had their buttons arranged in pairs, with a space between them.

○ Light Infantry Company

In 1771, Gen. William Howe, Commander of the Regular British Army in North America formed a Light Infantry Battalion from each regiment in America.

These were some of the more physically fit and usually younger soldiers.

These usually wore a shorter coat, gaitered trousers, and more practical hats rather than the standard cocked hat.

These soldiers were issued muskets with shorter rifled barrels, which were more accurate than the ones carried by the hat companies. Those muskets are referred to today as the 2nd Model Brown Bess.

Light Infantry companies were considered Flank Companies. Unlike the Hat Companies, they did not advance across a field and attack the enemy directly in rows. These were sent out as scouts or advance troops and were to attack the enemy on their side, which is called *flanking the enemy*.

○ Grenadiers

Gen. Howe also formed on Battalion of Grenadiers from each regiment.

These were usually taller soldiers. They wore tall bearskin hats which made them look even taller and more intimidating.

Prior to the Revolution they carried a primitive form of a grenade.

2. Dragoons

Dragoons were regiments of soldiers in the Regular British Army who were mainly on horseback. They are called Cavalry today.

Not all members of a Dragoon Regiment were on horseback; some were on foot.

These wore short coats and leather caps with horsehair plumes.

Most wore longer swords and a pistol or a carbine, which is a shorter form of a musket.

There is a great need for more people to do this impression.

3. Royal Artillery

Unlike the Continental Army, the Royal Artillery was separate from the Infantry. It had different requirements for its members. They all had to read and be able to solve mathematical equations. Members were required to attend Artillery School. And unlike the Regular Army its members could work their way up from being an enlisted man to become an officer.

Unlike the Infantry, the Artillery on both sides usually wore the same uniform. They wore blue coats faced in red with gold/yellow lace around plain brass buttons. They wore cocked hats with yellow/gold trim.

The 3rd and 4th Battalion of Royal Artillery were dispatched to the colonies. Later in the war the 3rd Battalion wore felt caps with red horsehair plumes, similar to the Dragoons, The 4th Battalion then wore caps with racoon tails on top.

Unlike regiments of Regular Soldiers, Royal Artillery did not field together as a regiment. Gun crews were dispatched as field artillery to go to battle with Infantry Regiments.

4. Royal Navy

The Royal Navy is a very underrepresented element in reenacting. Like the Artillery, the Navy usually wore the same uniform on both sides. The officers wore dark blue coats. The seamen usually wore sloops and a shorter coat.

5. Loyalists

Those in America who sided with the Crown during the Revolution were known as *Loyalists* or *Royalists*.

Local Militia answered to the Colonial Assemblies, so once Independence was declared and Local Militia opposed the Crown, many loyal to the Crown in America and Canada formed Royal Provincial Regiments.

Those regiments were provided uniforms and accoutrements like the

Regular Army. At first they were generally issued white small clothes and green regimental coats with buttons which had a crown and the letter RP for Royal Provincial. Later many Loyalists had red regimental coats.

During the Revolution these were sometimes called *Patriots* by those from England because the United Kingdom was their country. That term later was used by Americans to denote those who opposed the Crown.

These were often called *Tories* by the colonists. Tories were a political party in England which supported putting down the Revolution.

6. Germanic Troops

Troops from what would later be called Germany served under the Crown. There were two types: Hessians and Jagers.

○ Hessians

Propaganda portrayed these soldiers as mercenaries. That was not true. They were part of a feudal system and ordered to go as part of an agreement between German Lords and the German King George III who sat on the English throne.

Hessians usually wore blue regimental coats faced with buff. Some wore cocked hats; others wore tall mitre caps with elaborately embossed brass.

○ **Jagers**

They word Jager means *Hunter* in German. Jagers were more of a Light Infantry. They often served as Rangers. Most wore short green regimental coats faced in red. Unlike the Hessians, they caried rifles which were much smaller than the standard musket and had rifled barrels. That made them a more deadly accurate weapon but took longer to load.

Jagers were one of the few types of soldiers in the Revolution who had facial hair. Mustaches were common on Jagers.

9. Surgeons

The Regular British Army had surgeons accompany them to treat the wounded or sick soldiers.

Sometimes they had to perform amputations because of serious wounds.

What Did They Wear?

General Appearance

Here are some important general things about appearance, which apply to most soldiers who served in the Revolutionary War.

1. Facial Hair

During the 18th Century most men were clean shaven, even mountain men, and pirates. It is okay for a soldier to have three days of growth when on campaign.

Some evidence suggests some prisoners, and people classified back then as insane, were the only groups with facial hair.

Regarding facial hair, Hessian and French soldiers were an exception, many had a mustache.

Many reenactors, like my brother, usually have facial hair but shave it off to look more accurate for events. It usually grows back.

2. Hair

The Crown Forces required all men to have their hair long enough to be tied in a cue (like a ponytail tied up in a bun at the end).

In the colonies, the length of hair varied. Many followed the British custom of long hair and some wore wigs.

As the seeds of unrest grew before the Revolution many in the colonies showed their rebellion by cutting their hair short. Gen. William Howe referred to New Yorkers as a bunch of *Roundheads*, without a hair on their heads longer than an inch.

Shortly after the Battle of New York in 1776, Gen. Howe ordered his troops to cut their hair short. Probably due to the abundance of lice in New York. When Gen. Cornwallis later assumed command, he ordered them to regrow their hair.

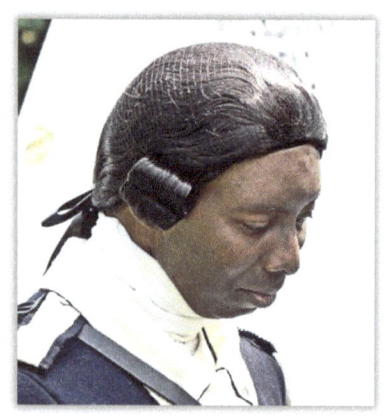

3. Wigs

Officers, and many older civilians, often wore wigs. That was easier to maintain than their own hair and it always looked good.

Some cut their hair very short, so their wigs fit better. Some

men allowed some of their natural hair to show when wearing their wigs. That was to show they were clearly wearing a wig, which let people know they were affluent enough to afford one.

Enlisted men did not wear wigs.

4. Eyeglasses

Eyeglasses were extremely expensive and worn by very few. They were mainly used for reading.

No reliable documentation has been found yet which shows they were worn by soldiers in the ranks when fielding.

Our unit recommends if someone needs corrective eyewear for a distance that they wear contacts.

Some good units allow members to field with glasses if they are period correct.

Some buy the round colonial sunglasses from Jas. Townsend and have their prescription lenses installed in those frames.

5. Hand-sewn Clothing

There were no sewing machines at that time, so all clothing was hand-sewn. A lot of that sewing was so fine it would be mistaken today for machine sewn.

Many reenactors use sewing machines to sew seams which do not show. Some like me, only d hand sweing.

Larry A. Maxwell

Small Clothes
The Foundational Garments

All men, both civilians and soldiers, wore small clothes. Small clothes are the foundational items for all impressions. You were considered undressed unless you were wearing all these items.

Small Clothes consisted of a shirt; socks; pants; and a waistcoat.

Unless you are joining a specific unit which requires otherwise, I recommend you choose white small clothes, as that is what most soldiers wore. That will allow you to easily switch between some historically accurate military looks.

1. Shirt

Soldiers in the Crown Forces, and most Continental soldiers, wore a shirt which was usually a long-sleeved knee-length white linen pullover shirt. Linen was an inexpensive fabric. Some richer people might have a cotton or silk shirt.

Militia could have shirts other than white. Some had ones with small red and white checks, or blue and white checks.

Some people only owned one or two shirts. They often slept in the shirt they wore during the day.

The neck of most shirts was secured with two thread buttons. The cuffs of the sleeves on most shirts were very narrow and had simple cufflinks.

2. Socks

Men and women wore long knit socks, usually made of wool. They extended above the knees. These were usually held up by means of a set of leather garters, secured by small buckles.

3. Pants

Different styles of pants were worn by those who served in the Revolution.

What Did They Wear?

○ **Breeches**

Back during the French & Indian War most men wore knee-length, French Button Fly Breeches. The buttons were in the front center. By the Revolutionary War fashion changed. Though older men may still have the French Button Fly style most wore the newer Drop-front style. That style continued through the War of 1812.

Breeches extended just below the knee. They were worn snug on the legs and had an abundance of material in the rear.

These were made of linen, sailcloth (cotton or linen canvas), wool, or leather.

These were cinched by means of ties in the back. Belts were not worn to hold these up. Sometimes a small flap was sewn inside the waistcoat to attach to the front middle button of the breeches to help hold them up.

○ **Trousers**

Some soldiers wore trousers. They had the same design as the Drop Front Style Breeches, but they extended to the shoes. Some were straight cut, some extended over the shoes, Some wore gaitered trousers where the lower part of the trousers was shaped like a gaiter which buttoned on the outside.

○ **Slops**

Most seamen on both sides wore slops. These were like breeches with wide, loose bottoms. These were usually made of sail cloth.

They were often solid white or had a ticking pattern of blue and white alternating stripes.

4. Waistcoat

The waistcoat was usually made of linen, wool, cotton, or silk. Each regiment had uniform specifications for the material to use.

The waistcoat extended below the waist and usually had two points. Some had lacing up the back to help with size adjustments.

These became shorter and were often cut straight across for Light Infantry and by some other units later in the war.

5. Neckwear

Most men wore a neck stock or a silk neck scarf around their neck.

○ **Neck Stock**

Most neck stocks were about 70" long. Many were made of white linen or white or colored silk. These were wrapped around the neck and tied in the front.

Some regiments used leather neck stocks or neck stocks made with black horsehair.

○ **Silk Neck Scarf**

Many Militia and some soldiers in the Continental Army wore Silk Neck Scarves. These went around the neck and were tied in front.

Footwear

Footwear is an especially important part of a historical impression. Not only is footwear practical, but many will look at your feet to see what you are wearing. You should NOT wear modern footwear.

Most people wore black leather shoes during the Revolution but there were some other types of footwear worn.

1.   Shoes

- **Black Leather Shoes**

Black leather shoes with brass or silver buckles were standard footwear. Some lower classes had simple laces. Some wore straight last shoes where there was neither a left nor right shoe. Both shoes were cut the same. They formed to the wearer's feet.

If you are doing an Apprentice Level Impression, in some cases it is possible to hide modern shoes by using gaiters. You must wear plain black leather shoes for that to work. Some people buy those shoes at thrift stores.

- **Jefferson Bootees**

These were a higher cut black leather shoe. There is some evidence to suggest some wore these. They are similar to Civil War Brogans.

- **Moccasins**

In some remote areas some wore center-seamed moccasins, especially those who interacted with Tribal People.

- **Riding Boots**

Dragoons and officers often wore tall black leather riding boots. The tops were often folded down revealing the inside brown undyed leather.

- **Spatterdash/Gaiters**

Most Crown Forces and some regiments of Continental Soldiers wore these. Each regiment had a uniform style for these. Some went as high as the knee. Some wore half-gaiters. Some were white, some were black.

These protected your ankles. They can be used to hide modern shoes for a casual or Apprentice look.

- **Wooden Shoes**

Wooden shoes can be correct for Militia or Civilians who do some impressions with Dutch connections such as New York and Northern New Jersey.

- **Bare Feet or Cloth Wrapped Feet**

Many times during the war supplies ran low. Shoes wore out and no replacements were available. Bare feet or cloth wrapped feet can be historically correct for some impressions or time periods.

Headwear

All men wore hats most of the time, even indoors. They were made of wool felt or beaver. If you want to get only one thing to start, I recommend a hat.

Hats can be one of the easiest things to make.

1. Floppy Hat

The Floppy Hat was the most common basic hat. It had an oval crown and a wide brim. This was one of the most practical hats as it provided shade from the sun and protection from the rain.

Sometimes the back or one side was cocked up.

What Did They Wear?

2. Round Hat

The Round Hat was another common hat. It was a Floppy Hat with the brim cut back uniformly to about 3-4". This was more practical than the tricorn or cocked hat because it provided some protection from the sun and rain. Sometimes one side was cocked up.

Sailors often wore Round Hats with Narrow brims.

3. The Tricorn

This hat was the fashion statement of the day. It is a very impractical hat. It is a floppy hat with three sides cocked up and attached to the crown in a triangular fashion.

This was a common civilian hat. Sometimes it was embellished on the left side with a cockade. If it were used by the military it would have a cockade and a button on the wearer's left side.

4. Cocked Hat

This hat is similar to a tricorn but is different in that it is less triangular. There is more of gap between the two sides and back. These were worn by the Regulars, most Continentals, and many Militia members.

The edge was usually trimmed with black or white. Artillery hats were trimmed in yellow.

For military use these were embellished with a cockade as well as a standard military button.

Unlike the civilian tricorn, who wore their hat with the center point between the eyes, soldiers wore these with the center point over the left eye, so the hats were out of the way when a musket was in the shoulder position.

5. Caps

Caps were usually worn by light infantry and some artillery. They were often made of leather.

Wool felt ones were made by cutting off the brim of a floppy hat. Some left the front of the brim as a visor. Many used an emblem on a separate upright front piece.

6. Canadian & Knits Caps

During the Canadian Campaign of 1775, some Continental Soldiers adopted the warm Canadian Caps for cold weather. Some were red wool caps trimmed with animal fur.

Many Seamen and Militia and Some Continentals wore knit caps.

7. Dragoon Helmets

During the Revolutionary War there were regiments of mounted soldiers called Dragoons on both sides.

Some members of Dragoon Regiments were on foot.

They usually wore hard leather helmets crested with either horsehair or fur.

8. Grenadier Hats

Most regiments in the Crown Forces had a Company of Grenadiers. These were usually taller soldiers who looked very intimidating because they wore 12" tall bearskin hats which made them look even taller. Some Fusiliers wore a slightly different version of these.

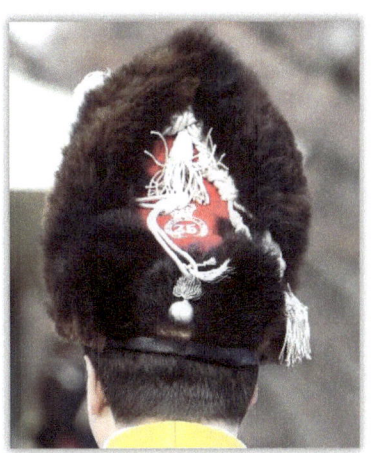

9. Hessians Mitre Caps

Hessians were troops from what later became known as Germany. They were part of the Crown Forces.

They were not mercenaries. They were still part of a feudal system and sent by their landlord overseers.

Most soldiers in Hessian Regiments wore tall miter caps with elaborately embossed brass plates on the front.

10. Straw Hats

Women and some men wore some straw hats. They were different than modern straw hats.

Larry A. Maxwell

Outerwear

Outerwear are the items worn over the Small Clothes.

1. Frock Coat

The Frock Coat was one of the most common outer garments worn by men in Colonial Times. These were usually made from wool. Some were made from a heavier linen.

These were simple or elaborate, depending on one's social standing. They all swept away above the waist and had a split seam in the back. The lower fronts of the coats were often fastened to the back forming two tails.

Some had working buttons and working pockets. Some only had decorative buttons and pocket flaps. Some had lapels, most did not. A few had decorative buttons on the cuffs.

A frock coat, waistcoat, and breeches made of the same fabric and color, was called a *Ditto Suit*. That was more common for the upper middle class.

2. Regimental Coat

The military wore frock coats called Regimental Coats. The Regimental Coat was designed more as a fashion statement rather than as a practical garment. They swept away before they reached the waist.

Most had lapels with non-working buttonholes. Those usually closed at the top by means of two or three sets of hooks and hoops. Some Regiments Coats had working buttonholes, particularly towards the end of the war.

What Did They Wear?

During the French & Indian War Regimental Coats extended down to the knees. By the time the Revolution started they were shortened to reach above the knee and were sometimes referred to as *Short Coats* (pictured to the left). That can cause confusion for some reenactors because Light Infantry Coats can also be called Short Coats and are a very different style. These were usually straight across the front and back. They resemble a waistcoat with sleeves. Sometimes they are called *Coates* (pictured below).

Each regiment had its own color coat and a specific-colored facing. Most had matching buttons on each label, some buttons bore regimental markings. Most had non-working buttons. They were lined partially, or fully, in linen or shalloon.

Some units had different style coats issued during the war. During the Burgoyne Campaign, which started in Canada and extended down to Saratoga, New York, most regimental coats for the Crown Forces were cut down to be shorter which was more practical in the forests the troops often went through.

Generals and Colonels bought and designed their own Regimental Coats, with the same colors as their men.

3. Hunting Frock/Shirt

The Hunting Frock/Shirt was a fringed white, brown, or solid colored outer garment often worn by hunters or woodsmen in the South or in the Frontier.

These were often made from a heavy white linen or sail cloth. They had attached capes of the same material edged with fringe to help repel water. Fringe was often attached to the sleeves, cuffs and a cape.

Back during the French & Indian War, British officers noticed the men wearing these, who were often good shots because they were hunters from Virginia or Pennsylvania. Some think that was the main reason, when General Washington was put in charge of the Continental Army, he ordered the army to wear them.

Many regiments in the South wore them but most in the North had no idea what these were. Most regiments did not get them at first. Some northern regiments got them later in the war.

These are simpler to make and less costly than a Regimental Coat.

5. Work Shirt

Many farmers and laborers wore work shirts over their regular shirt when they did work. Many Militia wore these.

Work shirts are made the same way as a regular shirt but are of a more durable material such as wool, heavy linen, sail cloth, or oil cloth. These were sometimes referred to as *Hunting Shirts* in the Northeast.

6. Great Coat & Blankets

Soldiers did not have any garments issued for cold weather. Some acquired long wool Great Coats, sometimes called *Watch Coats*.

Some took blankets, folded then in half, in the shape of a triangle, and put that over their shoulders.

Musicians

Musicians were an important part of the army. Each regiment on both sides had fifers and drummers. Some had buglers and pipers.

Musicians varied in age from as young as eight years old and up. In 1775, the 4th NY Regiment had a drummer who was 70 years old.

On both sides Musicians usually wore the same small clothes as the regiment they were with.

The main difference between a regular soldier's uniform and a musician's uniform was the musicians wore the reverse colors of the unit. A regiment which wore red coats faced white had musicians wear white coats faced red.

In the Crown Forces the exception to that was musicians in Royal Regiments did not wear reverse colors. Such as the Royal Artillery. There were also some American units in the early war where musicians did not wear reverse colors, such as the New York Regiments in 1775.

Most musicians had fancy lacing on their sleeves and other parts of their regimental coats.

Drummers wore a drum carriage. It was a black or white leather belt worn over the right shoulder. It had a hook for holding the drum. It also had a piece of leather on the front which served as a holder for the drumsticks.

Fifers wore a fife holder. A leather belt was worn over the left shoulder which held a cylindrical brass fife holder.

All the musicians wore swords. According to the 1768 Clothing Warrant for the Crown Forces, musicians were to wear swords after the scimitar fashion.

Larry A. Maxwell

Military Accoutrements

Militia and most soldiers, while not on duty, generally wore small clothes, an outer garment, and a hat. When in service, they wore a cartridge box/pouch, a bayonet sling/belt, a canteen, a haversack, and some kind of bed roll or backpack. Some wore swords.

Belts, for holding up pants, were not part of men's clothing yet. Sometimes a loop was sewn inside the waistcoat which would button to the breeches to help hold up pants.

1. Cartridge Box/Pouch

Crown Forces and Continental Soldiers had standard cartridge boxes to hold a certain number of pre-made cartridges for their muskets, as well as extra flints and a musket tool.

Militia usually had their own personal boxes or pouches in different styles.

2. Bayonet Sling/Belt

The bayonet sling or belt held the bayonet for the musket for the British Regular or Continental Soldier. Most were worn over the shoulder. Some were worn around the waist.

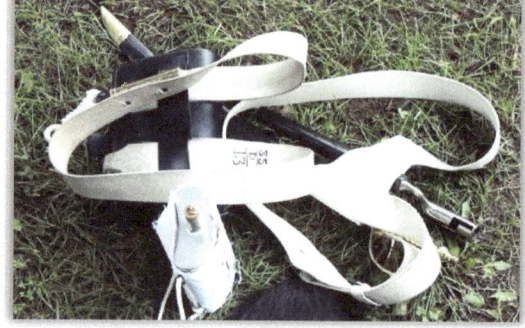

Some held both a bayonet and a sword or tomahawk.

The Militia usually did not have bayonets. Some had plug bayonets or tomahawks which were held in a sling.

3. Canteens

Crown Forces and most Continental soldiers used uncovered tin canteens. Covering canteens with wool cloth did not occur until the War Between the States.

Some Continentals and many Militia used wood canteens. Some militia used canteens made from gords or old bottles.

4. Haversacks

Haversacks were a standard issued item worn by all soldiers. They were primarily used to hold a soldiers' rations. These were worn high on the left side.

Reenactors often use these to hold their cup, plate, spoon, wallet, cell phone, snack, keys, and other miscellaneous items.

5. Knapsacks/Backpacks/ Blanket Rolls

Knapsacks, Backpacks and/or Blanket Rolls were worn on campaign. These held personal items such as an extra shirt, sewing kit, extra shoes, and a blanket. These were usually standardized for Regulars and Continental Soldiers.

Local Militia Laws required most Militia to have some of these items including a knapsack. Many probably followed a standard pattern but they were not standardized for Milita.

6. Powder Horn

Riflemen, some Militia, and some Artillery, who did not carry rolled cartridges, wore Powder Horns with black powder.

Continental & Regular Soldiers generally did not use Powder Horns. There was no need for them to carry them as they carried pre-rolled cartridges which contained both powder and a musket ball. The soldier would bite off the end of the cartridge, pour some powder in the pan as primer and then ram the rest down the barrel.

7. Swords

Most of the thirteen colonies had Militia Laws before the Revolution. Some Militia Laws, like the one in New York, required every member of the militia to own a firelock (musket) and a sword. Muskets cost almost a month's wage. Few owned them. When they went to drills, many used long wooden muskets. On the other hand, many owned swords and wore them frequently, even when not called to service.

On June 14, 1775, the Continental Congress formed the Continental Army. Each colony was called upon to form Continental Line Regiments. New York formed four. Of the 300 men from the east side of the Hudson River who joined the 4th New York Regiment, only 70 owned muskets but most owned swords. Usually, only officers and musicians wore swords but in 1775, many privates in the 4th New York Regiment wore their swords.

Throughout the war, all officers, artillery, mounted troops, and most musicians wore swords.

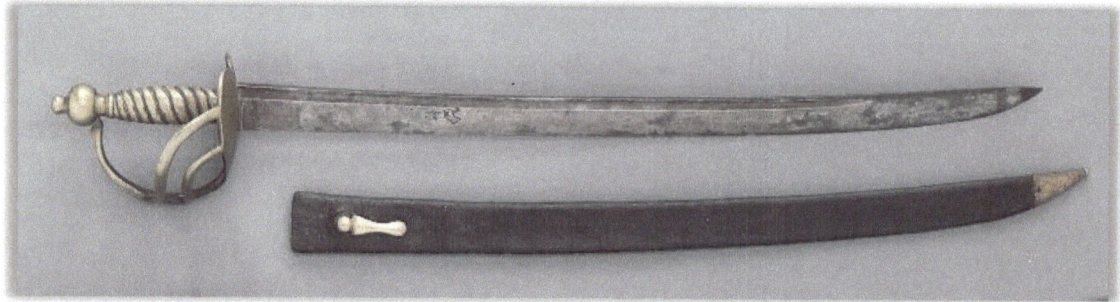

The above pictured 1751 British Hanger was a common sword used during the Revolution.

8. Sash

A sash was worn around the waist by some corporals, all sergeants, and by most officers except generals. This was standard in the Continental Army and Crown Forces. Some Militia officers also used sashes.

9. Epaulette

Epaulettes were part of some uniforms and were worn on the shoulder. They were also used by both sides to indicate rank.

The 1768 Clothing Warrant gave orders about epaulettes for the Regular British Army.

Gen. Washington ordered Noncommissioned Officers and Regular Officers in his army to

wear an epaulette on their shoulder to identify their rank. It was a simple colored piece of cloth worn on one shoulder. Some regiments choose not to follow that order.

Many Captains, Lieutenants and Colonels wore more elaborate epaulettes. Many Generals only wore one epaulette.

Larry A. Maxwell

How to Acquire
The Necessary Items for an Impression

As you determine the look you want to achieve, the big question is where do you get those items? There are a few ways to acquire them.

1.   Borrow Things

Our reenacting unit, and some other units, let people who are interested in reenacting with us borrow items to get started. That lets them get involved right away to see if they really want to do this. Then we help them get a good look.

Borrowing items is highly recommended for young people who are still growing. It is best to pass on items as members grow up.

2.   Make Things

Making things is one of the best ways to save money and get a more historically accurate look. You do not initially need to know how to sew to do this. You just need to be willing to learn and get good advice from people who know what they are doing.

When I started reenacting I bought basic pre-made small clothes. I then decided to try to make the other items I needed. That meant I needed to learn how to sew.

The first item I made was a Hunting Frock done following a pattern in *Sketch 76: The American Soldier 1775-1781*. I had no idea how to sew. Today you can find out how to do that on the internet but that was back before the internet was popular. I went to my local library to take out a book on sewing. I discovered my library did not have any books on sewing. So, I went to a local grocery store and asked some women standing in line if they would show me how to do some basic stitches. A few graciously replied. They drew illustrations on some paper grocery bags showing me how to do some stitches. I used that advice, and hand sewed the hunting frock. I then wore that Hunting Forck I made to the 225th Anniversary of the Battle of White Plains, New York.

It did not take long for me to discover the small clothes I initially bought were okay for an Apprentice look but were not historically accurate enough to be close to the public. One of the best things that happened to me was Phil Weaver, of

Continental Consulting, leader in the 2nd NY Regiment and one of the finest Colonial Tailors, taught me how to make historically correct items.

Before reenacting I never considered sewing. I was surprised when I later discovered my great grandfather James Maxwell, who came to America from Scotland, was a tailor, as was his father and some of my other ancestors.

I learned how to hand sew shirts, waistcoats, regimental coats, hats, breeches, haversacks, tents, cartridge boxes, sword carriages, and much more. I even learned how to make some women's clothing for my daughters.

3. Get Things at Reenactments

Reenactments are a particularly good place to acquire items. Sutlers and some reenactors make items and then sell them at reenactments. The good thing is that way you get to see and handle the items in person before buying them.

Not all items for sale at events are historically accurate or appropriate for your impression. Make sure you have a knowledgeable person to assist you in your shopping.

4. Get Used Reenactor Clothing

You can save some time and money by getting used clothing, modifying them, and adjusting them to fit you.

Some reenactments have blanket sales where reenactors sell used items. That is one of the best-priced places to buy used items for the best prices. Make sure you have someone knowledge about your impression to assist you.

Some reenactors sell items online which no longer fit. Some also leave the hobby and sell their items online on a Facebook Page or on eBay. Those can provide great buys. You may want to consider making an Items Wanted Posting.

5. Online Sutlers

You can buy some items, and put together a good Apprentice look, and possibly a Journeyman Look by buying items from some Online Sutlers. Again, make sure you have a knowledgeable person assist you. Some Online Sutlers are better with historical authenticity than others.

Larry A. Maxwell

Making Your Own Items

You can save a lot of money if you make your own items. You do not need to know how to sew, you can learn. I had no idea how to sew when I first started.

It can be expensive to buy historically accurate items. Consider the cost of buying the proper materials, plus the cost of the labor to make each item. Currently it costs me between $160-250 on average for correct materials to make one regimental coat. Those figures are constantly changing.

It is also important to make sure the garments you make fit properly. A well-made but wrongly fitting garment does not portray history correctly.

Everything was hand sewn during the Revolution. That takes longer than using a sewing machine. It takes me about 20 hours to hand sew a shirt, about 40 hours to hand sew a waistcoat, and about 60 hours to hand sew a regimental coat, without lace.

What would be a fair price to pay for a historically accurate hand sewn item? Multiply the hours it takes to make an item by a reasonable hourly wage for a craftsman to make something. If you figured $20 an hour, which is extremely low, multiply that by the number of hours it takes to make an item. Then add to that figure the current cost of the correct materials to make each item.

So, what would be a fair price to expect to pay to buy a historically accurate hand sewn regimental coat today? If you figure the minimum cost of materials is $160 and add to that the minimum labor cost of 60 hours to make simple coat and multiply that by $20 per hour, that equals $1,200. The total lowest cost for one hand sewn regimental coat would be a minimum of $1,360. If you find someone selling a regimental coat for less than that, consider that a great bargain.

More than ten years ago, one of the good Revolutionary War tailors, who used a sewing machine to sew all unseen seams, told me he charged a minimum of $2,000 per regimental coat.

I hand sew everything but many use sewing machines to sew all seams which do not show. That reduces labor costs to produce an item. That works fine for the Apprentice and Journeyman looks and is accepted by the Big Three reenacting organizations.

If you are portraying a Regular Solider in the Crown Forces, or Artillery on either side, or a Musician, it will cost more for your regimental coat because you must add the cost of the lace required for those coats. Each regiment uses specific lace. That is applied around each button, and on the back, and on the shoulders for Light Infantry, on the sleeves for musicians, and is also used for epaulettes. You must also add the 20-40 additional hours needed to apply that lace to the coat.

That can be a good reason to buy used items, if available, and then modify them.

How Can You Learn to Make Historically Accurate Items?

O   Learn from a Knowledgeable Person

One of the best ways to learn many things is from a knowledgeable person. Some regiments have regimental tailors who might be willing to teach you. If they do not, they should be able to recommend someone who might be able to teach you.

I was honored to have one of the best Regimental Tailors, Phil Weaver of Continental Consulting, graciously spent many hours teaching me how to make historically accurate Revolutionary War clothing.

Larry A. Maxwell

○ Attend Workshops

Some regiments and historic sites periodically hold workshops to teach people how to make historically accurate items. I highly recommend you attend one or more.

Some of the best workshops for learning how to make quality historically accurate clothing are taught by Henry Cooke.

Henry Cooke of Historical Costume Services conducts numerus workshops throughout the year in various places. I attended one of his workshops and it was a great learning experience.

The cost to attend his workshop sometimes includes a historically correct pattern and historically correct materials to make each item. He also teaches participants the proper fit for the garments.

○ Watch YouTube Videos

There are many videos on YouTube which you can watch to learn how to make historically accurate Revolutionary War clothing. Some are good, some are not.

○ Contemporary Artwork

The fact there was no photography in the Revolutionary War makes paintings and sketches by artists, during that period one of the most helpful resources for determining what people made and wore.

○ Newer Artwork & Statues

There is some good artwork and statutes produced by artists who are also researchers.

Ron Tunison and Michael Keropian are two outstanding sculptors who I had the privilege of knowing. Both did meticulous research for each monument they were commissioned to produce. I provided some research for Keropian for his monument of Wappinger Sachem Daniel Nimham, who gave his life fighting alongside his son Abraham Nimham during the Revolution.

Don Troiani is a collector of military artifacts and an excellent painter. He does paintings of military characters based on his research. Much of what he does is very accurate. He has compiled many of his painting in books.

⭕ Visit Museums

It is extremely helpful to look at surviving items from the period you want to portray. The sad thing is, there are few surviving garments from the Revolutionary War. Some surviving garments and artifacts are in museums where you can go see them. Some reproductions have been mislabeled as originals.

I was thrilled to see surviving garments and artifacts from the Revolution in the Military Museum at Edinburgh Castle in Scotland.

Many museums also have historically accurate reproductions. Some also house collections of military miniatures painted by meticulous researchers.

⭕ Read Books

When I became interested in reenacting I started buying books about Revolutionary War clothing. I usually buy those as used books on Amazon and always look for them at book sales.

Many books on the Revolutionary War have been written over the years. Some address what the soldiers wore. Some are helpful but some are too speculative. New research has rendered some books obsolete. I found many books in the Osprey Military Series extremely helpful.

The Company of Military Historians produces Journals with professionally researched reliable articles in every issue regarding military uniforms from different time periods. I looked around for back issues addressing specific Revolutionary War items I wanted to make. Phil Weaver authored some good articles published in those journals.

Larry A. Maxwell

Practical Pointers for Making Some Items

It takes time and effort to make things, but it can save money and is a rewarding experience. Many people can learn how to make historically accurate items.

Here are practical tips on how to make some historically accurate items for portraying a soldier or boy in the Revolutionary War.

Resizing a Hat

First determine if you can resize an existing hat. A simple way to make a wool felt hat larger is to put about 3" of water in a large pot. Bring the water to a boil. Hold the hat over the steam for a minute or two. Then, carefully screw the hat down on the head you want it to fit. Do not force it too much and be careful it will be hot. Wear it for about 10 minutes, then repeat the process again. I have transformed hats from small to large, or large to extra-large this way.

You can also make a hat smaller by inserting some material behind the hat liner.

Making a Hat

Making hats can be a complicated process. Technically you start with a wool felt millinery cone. That is then shaped into a wool felt capeline. Then you stiffen that and at that point it is called a hat blank. The hat blank is then lined and shaped into one of many style hats.

Millinery Cone

Capeline

Hat Blank

I start with either a 100% wool felt capeline or a hat blank. Quartermaster General or Jas. Townsend are a good source for hat blanks. You can buy them in different sizes and even buy ones with a hat liner or make the liner yourself.

Determine the size hat you need by measuring around the circumference of the wearer's head.

To make the liner, you will need linen material and tape/ribbon. Cut out the material in a rectangle with the long side being the circumference plus 2" and the other side being 3-5" depending on your preference.

Tape ribbon is usually used to tie the liner closed after it is attached near the crown of the hat. Cut the tape/ribbon the length of the circumference plus 6-8".

Fold the shorter edge twice, so the unfinished edge does not show. Sew along that seam with a running stitch. Do that for both sides.

Next, lay the ribbon along the long side and fold the material over it once, with about ¼" overlap. Then fold that over itself. Then sew along the edge of that

assembly just below the tape/ribbon using a running back stitch. Make sure you do not sew through the tape/ribbon. Your basic liner is now finished.

To attach the liner, locate the back center of the hat. Pin the unfinished long edge to the inside, just above the brim, with the fold of the liner you just sewed facing the center of the hat. Then attach the liner to the hat with a running stitch using silk thread the same color as the hat. Make any adjustments when you make it completely around. Then tie the hat liner. You have now made a Floppy Hat.

Fold up the back or side flap and attach that with either thread or tape/ribbon. Or fold up the back and two sides and attach them, you have a cocked hat. Some regiments had worsted wool herringbone tape sewn around the outside brim. Artillery wore yellow, some regiments had white, some had black. When you sew the tape aeound the brim of the hat, make sure most of the tape is on the outside. Sew the inside brim using the least amount of tape possible.

For a Round Hat cut the rim leaving about 3".

You can use chalk to draw a front bill on the brim, like on a baseball cap. You can then cut out the rest of the brim and take a piece of the wool felt you cut off and make a shield to attach to the front and you have a later war infantry cap. Or you can cut off the entire brim and then

make a shield from the material you cut off and you have a basic light infantry or artillery cap.

You should also attach a button to the left side for the regiment you are portraying. You can then make a cockade from horsehair fabric or silk and attach that.

Larry A. Maxwell

Making a Shirt

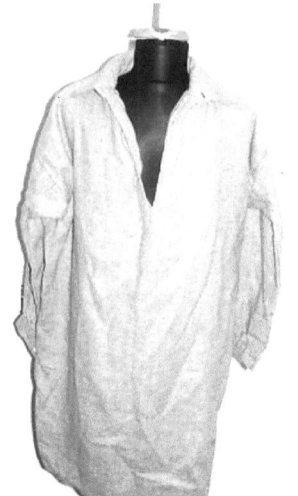

Everyone wore a shirt. Shirts are an easy garment to hand sew. You only need to know how to do a running stitch and a running back stitch. It is simply a matter of cutting out 12-14 correctly sized rectangles from linen and then sewing them together. When finished you add 2 buttonholes to the neck, preferably linen or silk thread buttons and 2 closures to the cuffs with either simple cuff links or buttons.

I recommend while you are first learning how to hand sew garments you make your first one out of less expensive cotton muslin or osnaburg. You can use that garment to make adjustments and then use it for a sleep shirt.

A Work Shirt is made the same way except using a heavier linen or wool. You can make these with oil cloth for a water-resistant outer garment.

The 12-14 rectangles for making a shirt are:

1 for the Body 36"x72"   2 for cuffs 3"x12.5"   2 for neck gussets 3"x3"
2 for sleeves 24"x24"   2-4 for sleeve gussets 6"x6"
1 for collar 8"x23"   2 for lower side body gussets 3"x3"

The length of the body and length of the collar are two of the most important measurements. The length of the sleeve is longer and one of the least important measurements as that adjusts when you secure the cuffs.

Fold the body piece in half. Find the center of the width of the body. Make a 10" line down the front of the body. Then carefully cut that line on the front only.

Measure 8-12" on each side perpendicular to the slit on the fold, depending on how large the neck of the person wearing the shirt will be. Then cut those two lines. Slightly fold in the front slit and sew it with a running back stitch.

The swe the sides of the body using a running back stitch, with double thread, on each side of the body starting 4-6" up from the bottom. Stop 12" before reaching the top.

Next, make the sleeves. First, sew the main part of each sleeve, using double thread, starting 6" from the end, which will be attached to the body, using a running back stitch. Stop 6" from the end where the cuffs will be attached.

Then place the sleeve gussets along the body end of the sleeve and attach them with double thread, using a running back stitch. Some people like to use two pieces for each sleeve gussets to strengthen a shirt.

Then make the cuffs for the sleeves. First you fold in each outside edge of the cuff, so the rough edges do not show. Sew that with a running stitch. Then fold the cuffs half width wise. Then fold in ½" along the long edge. Sew that with a single thread, using a running stitch. The cuffs should be narrow.

Then do a loose running stitch alone the cuff end of each sleeve. Then pull the thread so the sleeve end is gathered until it is the same size as the cuff you made. Place the sleeve inside of the folded cuff. Attach the cuff to the sleeve 1/2" from the end, using a single thread with a running stitch.

Next you attach the sleeves to the body using a running back stitch. Remember you are doing all of this with the shirt inside out. I like to attach the gusset part to the body flat, then run a thread through the rest of that end of the sleeve to create a gathered shoulder, then attach that with the same running back stitch.

Next, take the small neck gussets and attach them to the left and right neck slit you previously cut, using a running back stitch with double thread.

To make the collar, fold in the ends slightly and sew them with a running stitch. Then fold the collar in half along the width, Then, like you did with the cuffs, fold in the cut edges and secure them with a single thread, with a running stitch.

Now the collar is ready to attach. First, I make 3 to 5 pleats in the back and one on each side in the font. Then I pin the collar in place with the top shirt edge placed inside the folded collar. Then I adjust the pleats. Then with the shirt right side out, I attach the collar with a double thread, with a running stitch.

To complete the shirt in one of the more period correct manners, you sew two buttonholes in the neck on the left side and attach 2 small thread buttons on the right. You then make a buttonhole on each side of the cuffs and use correct cuff links to secure them. Wm. Booth Draper has a video on YouTube showing how to make the thread buttons. We have been converting all our shirts to those. Some people use one metal or bone button on the neck and cuffs.

When you finish sewing the shirt you can take an extra step and flat fell the seams. That means you fold the seams in the body and arms, so the rough edges are covered then do a tight running stitch on the inside close to the folded edge.

This same procedure for making a man's shirt can be adapted **To Make a Chemise for a Woman**. The lower portion of the body will sweep out. You eliminate the attacked collar and make a folded neckline with a linen ribbon to tie it closed. You also eliminate the cuffs and end with shorter wider sleeves which and are folded over on the rough ends. Two long triangular pieces are sewn on the lower portion of each side.

Making a Waistcoat

A waistcoat is part of the small clothes. It is a garment worn by all men during the Revolution, both civilians and military. This is a bit more complicated to make. It takes me about 40 hours to hand sew one. The length of time depends on what you line this with. Some linings are made with four pieces, the same as the body. Some are made with eight pieces which takes more time.

Determine the correct material for making a waistcoat for your impression. They were usually made of linen or wool, sometimes silk. When you make your first one I recommend you make it out of white linen. You can then use that for many impressions. Even those whose uniform required them to have a wool waistcoat most likely had a linen one for off duty or civilian wear.

Make sure you use an approved pattern for your impression

One of the problems you will encounter if you do re-enact for a long time is waistcoats always seem to shrink, or our bodies seem to grow larger in the mid-section. That makes waistcoats more difficult to button. One historical solution is to split the back seam of the waistcoat and add lacing. Some wait until that is needed to do that. Some like to do that in advance. In a regiment like mine this is an extremely helpful feature for the waistcoats because we lend them to new recruits and that helps them properly fit a wider range of people.

Basic Pieces for a Waistcoat

Making a Regimental Coat

Regimental Coats are part of the uniform for all Crown Forces, Continentals, and most soldiers, except for Militia (though some wore older ones they owned).

It takes me about 60 hours to hand sew a basic Continental Regimental Coat. Those usually have no lace and non-working buttons.

Most Crown Forces Regimental Coats have lace around the buttons. That requires buying a roll of lace and then making the 38 rectangles of lace which go around the buttons on the facings, cuffs, and on the back of the coat. Those have to be applied to the coat. That usually takes me an additional 20 hours.

If you make a Musicians Regimental Coat, they usually have lacing on the sleeves and epaulettes. For our Artillery Musicians Coats, it takes more than twice the amount of lace as the buttons, plus it takes me another 20 hours to apply that.

Henry Cooke offers practical workshops on making Lottery Coats. I am sure he would help you learn how to customize your Regimental Coat.

If you can make a shirt and waistcoat you can make a Regimental Coat. They are not really that hard to make. I authored a separate book called *Making a Regimental Coat*. That is available on Amazon and Barnes & Noble.

Pattern Pieces Laid Out for an Early War Regimental Coat
Minus Facing Pieces which would usually be a different color wool

Larry A. Maxwell

These Images Show the Proper Fit of a Early War Regimental Coat
Photos by Larry A. Maxwell

Making a Frock Coat

A Frock Coat is a simpler version of a Regimental Coat without facings. These were the basic outer garment for a Civilian. They were worn by most Militia as they provided their own clothing.

They can have working buttonholes.

They are usually made of wool or heavy linen and sometimes silk. These can be simple or elaborate. Some fancier ones can have embroidery.

Stitches Illustrated

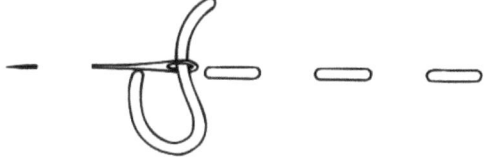

Running Stitch

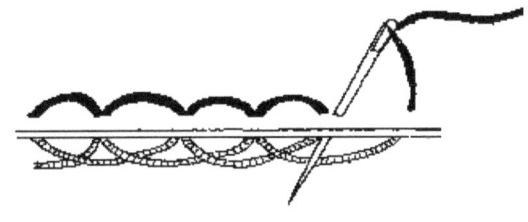

Running Backstitch

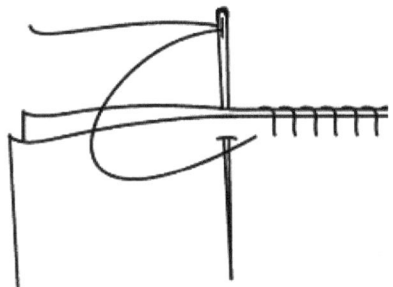

Whipstitch

Larry A. Maxwell

Sutlers

Sutlers is the name for the people who sell supplies to military reenactors. Some sell only at events, some sell only online, and some do both. Most sutlers sell items for many different impressions, and sometimes for different time periods. Some sell particularly good items; some sell low quality or historically inaccurate items.

Some sell items which are good for visitors at events, which are not designed for reenactors. It is important to understand, just because a sutler is at a good event does not mean you should buy what you need from them.

Here is VERY IMPORTANT advice, I highly recommend you DO NOT BUY from any sutler unless you have a knowledgeable person about the impression you want to do go with you.

At one event, where all the sutlers were pre-screened, one of our members went to a sutler and spent all his money buying socks which were period correct but not correct for our impression. He had a sign posted that said, "All Sales Final." He would not give him a refund.

If you are buying items online, you must have a knowledgeable person advise you BEFORE you make any purchase. It can be hard to determine the quality of an item online.

In this section I included a list of some sutlers I recommend for some items. This section is subject to change. Too often good sutlers go out of business.

For many years *Flying Canoe Traders*, from Quebec, Canada was one of my favorite sutlers. They primarily sold items for The French & Indian War but had great boiled wool blankets, and some other items. They also had a theatre and stage production company and sold used items at incredibly low prices.

Another favorite of mine was *Druid Oak*. He made very reasonable priced, good quality shirts, waistcoats, and hats. Sadly, he succumbed to cancer, and his business ceased operations.

When those two sutlers stopped doing business other sutlers significantly raised their prices once these competitors were gone.

The following are some good sutlers, for specific items, at the time this book was written. This is subject to change:

1. **Gossville Shoes – The BEST Shoes**
   GoosvilleNH.com Bruce & Penny Graham
   P.O. Box 772, 1758 Dover Rd., Epsom, NH 03234
   (603) 736-9044 Email: hidesmith@aol.com

Shoes are more important than some people may realize. Many people look at your feet to see what you are wearing. If you want to be historically correct you should make sure your footwear is correct.

Not only are shoes important for a good look but also for your own wellbeing. Poorly made shoes can have a negative health impact. I immediately noticed the difference when I started wearing the shoes made by Gossville Shoes.

Over the past 25 years I tried shoes from different suppliers. This is the man who makes the best shoes I ever owned. The cost for his shoes is much more than others but his shoes last longer and are of the highest quality. You must buy his shoes in person at events. He is often at the Battle of Monmouth Event in New Jersey and Battle of Newtown in New York.

2. Wm. Booth Draper – Fabric, Tape, Notions   WmBoothDraper.com
1365 Edgewood Dr., Lake Geneva, WI. 53147
262-203-5192

Paul from Wm. Booth Draper is a high quality, truly knowledgeable, helpful sutler. This is a good source for period correct fabrics, thread, some buttons, and notions.

We had the honor of having him field with us on our cannon crew at Old Sturbridge Village, Massachusetts.

He has good instructional videos on YouTube. I highly recommend watching the one on making thread buttons. I learned that from him and only use those type of buttons on all our shirts.

Sleeve Buttons (Cufflinks)

Linen Neck Stock

3. Roy Najecki Reproductions Buttons, Fabric, & More
Najecki.com   1203 Reynolds Rd., Chepachet, R.I. 02814

Roy Najecki has been both a reenactor and a subtler for many years.

He is a great source of quality items. He is a good source for correct buttons, buckles, fabric, regimental lace, and shoes.

We buy our buttons, buckles and regimental lace from Najecki. When I needed to make a Crown Forces General Coat he was the only one who sold the correct lace.

What Did They Wear?

Buttons

Kochan Wool

Regimental Lace

Doble D Buckle

All his fabric is historically accurate. If you want to make a regimental coat he sells the Kochan wool, which is the most accurate wool to use.

4. Brunley & Trowbridge
BrunleyandTrowbridge.com   P.O. Box 100, Valley Forge, PA. 19481

Good source for accoutrements, fabric, tape, notions, and pattens.

White Shirt Linen

Linen Twill Tape

J.P. Ryan Patterns

5. G. Gedney Godwin
GGGodwin.com   610-783-0670

Good source for shoe buckles, accoutrements, flints, flash guards, and many items for Crown Forces.

  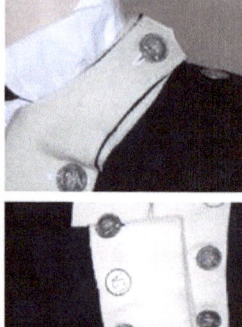 

Shoe Buckle   Regimental Coat   White Linen Breeches

6. Unites States Sword & Uniform
Gary Beauregard gcbussu@yahoo.com 732-616-4800

Gary Beauregard was a Field Artillery Major and retired from the military as a Lieutenant Colonel. He works with films and has been a reenactor since before the Bicentennial. He is Quartermaster for the New Jersey Sons of the American Revolution.

He is a quality individual who sells exceptionally good swords at very reasonable prices. Sometimes he has good Regimental Coats for a good buy.

He only sells at events or by phone contact. He does not have an online presence. Sometimes he sells on eBay.

7. Military Uniform Supply - Pants
MilitaryUniformSupply.com   309-346-1130

Good source for some clothing for the Apprentice and Journeyman looks, especially breeches and trousers. You will need to do some modifications to make them fit better. You should make sure you go over the visible seams with hand-titching.

What Did They Wear?

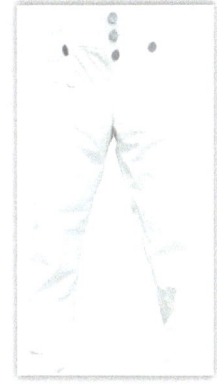

Breeches   Trousers

8.   Blockade Runner – Hat Blanks
BlockadeRunner.com 913-389-6294
1027 Bell Buckle/Wartrace Rd., Wartrace, TN 37183

Blockade Runner mostly sells Civil War items. However, they sell good thick hat blanks for a great price. I often use these to make hats.

9.   Townsends – Clothing, Hats
Townsends.US   800-338-1665
PO Box 415, 153 North First St., Pierceton, IN 46562

Townsends sells lots of durable clothing. They are all machine sewn. They sell shirts, waistcoats, regimental coats, socks, and hats. These are good for the Apprentice look. You will need to do hand stitching on visible seams for a Journeyman look. Or you can take them apart and re-hand sew them.

Hunting Frock | Linen Shirt | Regimental Coat

9. eBay Seller – Regimental Coats

Sometimes you can buy used Revolutionary War reenactors uniforms on Facebook Marketplace or on eBay.

There are some eBay sellers from Pakistan who make and sell decent well-made, reasonably priced regimental coats for under $200. That is almost what it cost me to buy the materials to make one. These are good for an Apprentice look. I modify these for a Journeyman look.

One seller's User Names is royal-military-jackets. I noticed sometimes users change their name. I look for the ones who sell through London, UK.

Some regiments who are members of the Continental Like and British Brigade order their regimental coats from this seller and then modify them.

What Did They Wear?

Historical Images

This book provides photographs of reenactors seeking to portray people from the Revolutionary War as historically accurate as they can. Photographs of actual people from the Revolution would be incredibly helpful but photography as we know it, was not developed until after the Revolution.

Historical paintings and sketches from the Revolutionary War are valuable in helping researchers determine what people wore back then. These images are provided for the reader to review and help them find details to help them do a better historically accurate portrayal.

THREE WARNINGS when using historical images.

FIRST, most artists have a bias and often use artistic license in their work.

This is true of paintings of some generals during the Revolutionary War.

Gen. William Howe
By Richard Purcell
Published May 10, 1778
National Portrait Gallery

David Wooster
By Thomas Hart
Published March 26, 1776
London

Notice how the portraits of Howe and Wooster look like the same person. Both artists painted these portraits without the subjects present. Richard Purcell was in London and did his painting of Howe while Howe was still in America. Thomas Hart was in London and never met or saw Wooster but did this work of him. All of Hart's portraits are considered fictitious.

It is important to remember Generals bought and designed their own uniforms. They usually had two different uniforms. One was worn for formal occasions. One was worn in the field. Their uniforms may have had similarities to the men who served with them, but they were usually more embellished.

General officers also wore uniforms similar but different than their men,

The SECOND WARNING is make sure the image was done during the Revolution by people who were there. Many paintings and sketches are contemporary with the Revolution but many, which people think were contemporary, were done many years later. Charles Peale painted many paintings of Revolutionary War figures, after the Revolution.

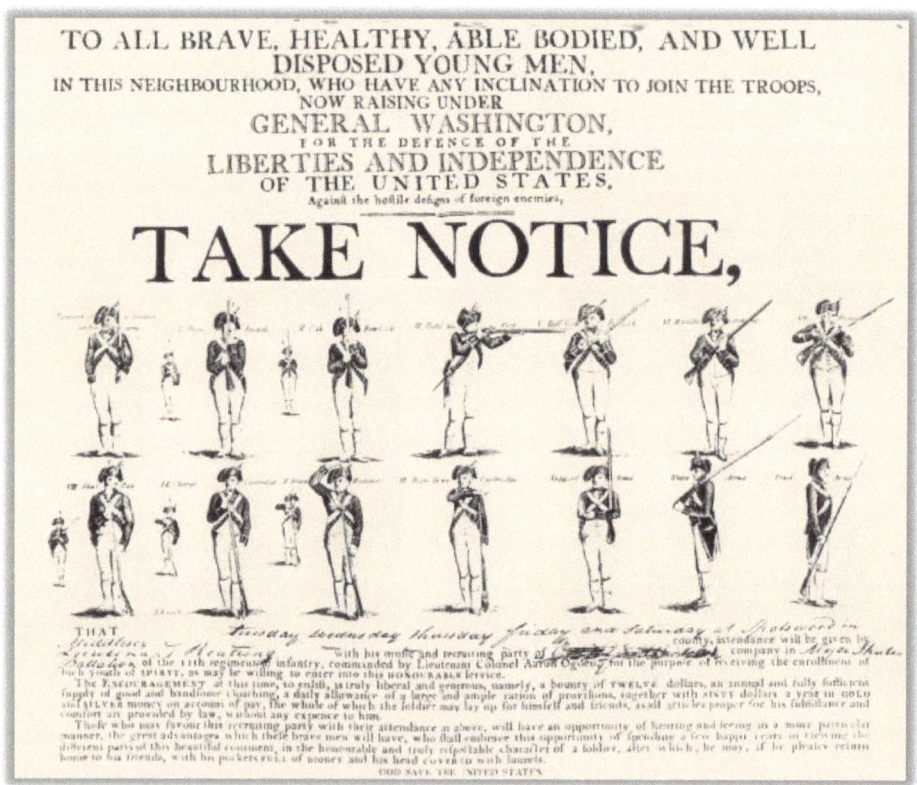

Recruiting Poster from After 1798 NOT From the Revolution
This poster is often shown in books as a Revolutionary War recruitment poster. This was not printed until after the war. The officers listed in this poster were members of the 11th Infantry Regiment which was not formed until 1798.
Printed by B. Jones, Philadelphia, 1798-1815

The THIRD WARNING is you need to make sure the subject is correctly identified.

For example, if you do an internet search for Sybil Ludington, the teenage female Paul Revere from the Hudson Valley of New York, almost every resulting image you will find is wrong. One of the most popular images provided is Eliza Izard Pinckney, wife of Thomas Pinckney. She managed one of the largest plantations of slaves in the South. Two miniatures were painted of her and her husband and are clearly labelled on the originals.

I have seen that picture of Eliza Pinckney sold in a gift shop in a museum as Sybil Ludington in Connecticut. When I showed them the proof this picture was not of Sybil Ludington the said they liked the image, it sold well, and they would still sell it as Sybil.

Eliza Izard Pinckney
By Edward Greene Malborne 1801
Charleston, S.C.

Sketch of Sybil Ludington
by Artcraft 1975
From Original Miniature

Three Classic Paintings

Here are three classic paintings people often reference when trying to put together a historical impression of the Revolutionary War. These are all great paintings but are artist conceptions painted many years after the Revolution.

Larry A. Maxwell

Washington Crossing the Delaware
Emanuel Leutze, Oil on Canvas, 1851. Metropolitan Museum of Art, New York

Presentation of the Declaration of Independence June 28, 1776
By John Trumbull 1818
Though Trumbull was not there. He included images of each signer for whom an official portrait existed. Some of then he included were not there but signed later.

What Did They Wear?

Spirit of '76 previously called **Yankee Doodle**
Painted in 1875 by Archibald M. Willard
Hangs in the Hall of Selectmen in Marblehead, Massachusetts
Called the World's Most Inspiring Patriotic Painting.
This was inspired by a parade Willard saw in Wellington, Ohio, honoring the Centennial Celebration of the Revolutionary War.
This painting is used as the basis for many who seek to portray characters from the Revolution. It is very accurate in some ways but not in others.

Larry A. Maxwell

Images of Battles in the Revolution

Look closely at what individuals wore in these images.

Death of General Montgomery at Quebec
John Trumbull, 1785 – *Painted 10 years after the Battle*
Yale University Art Gallery

Battle of Bunker Hill
By John Trumbull in the studio of Benjamin West – March 1786 London
Salem Poor is on the far right.
Published 11 Years After the Battle

What Did They Wear?

Death of General Mercer at the Battle of Princeton
By John Trumbull – Published 1787 – *11 Years after the Battle*
Yale University Art Gallery

Last Words of Captain Hanging of Captain Nathan Hale
Published in The History of New York City Vol. 3, M. Booth 1830
Image is Older Than the Book it Appeared in.

Larry A. Maxwell

Battle of Ridgefield
Published London Newspaper April 1780 – 3 years after the Battle
Original by R. Sayer & J. Benet - Colorized by Bryan Pratt

Francis Marion Crossing the Pee Dee River
William Tyler Ranney
Published 1852 – *Long after the Revolution*

What Did They Wear?

Soldiers at the Siege of Yorktown 1781

By Jean Baptiste Antoine de Verger a French soldier present at Yorktown,
1st R.I. Regt. on left - Anne S.K Brown Military Collection.

Surrender of Lord Cornwallis in 1781

By John Trumbull
Started Sketch in 1785 finished Painting 1819-1820

Larry A. Maxwell

Portraits of Those Who Served with the Crown Forces

Lord Hugh Percy
By Andres Van Rymsdyk 1777

Gen. Thomas Gage
By John Singleton Copley 1768

Lord Charles Cornwallis
by Daniel Gardiner 1783
Yorktown Foundation Collection

Gen. John Burgoyne
by Joshua Reynolds 1766
Frick Museum

Richard St. George 4th Regt. of Foot
By Thomas Gainsborough ca. 1776
Gallery Melbourne, Australia

John T. Rawdon-Hastings
Officer in the 15th Regiment of Foot
By John Trotter 1776 Dublin

Sir William Erskine
By Samuel William Reynolds
Col. Of the 80th Foot 1777

Wm. Blakeney
By Thoms Hill
23rd Reft, of Foot – Royal Welsh

John Graves Simcoe
By Jean-Laurent Mosnier
1791

Banastre Tarleton
By Josh Reynolds - 1782
National Gallery

Major John Andre
Drawn By Himself
Printed by H. B. Hall

Benedict Arnold
By Du Simitiere – Oct.3, 1780 Only In Person
Published in The European Magazine 1783

What Did They Wear?

Portraits of Tribal People from the Revolution

Key-On-Twog-Ky Cornplanter – Seneca
By F. Bartoli – ca. 1796

Sketch of Wappinger Stockbridge
By Capt. Johann Ewald 1778

Joseph Brant
By Gilbert Stuart
ca. 1784-1788

Portraits of Those Who Served with the Continentals

Daniel Morgan
By Charles W. Peale
National Park Service

George Washington
By Samuel King
Chateau Bierencourt Picardy

Horatio Gates
By Charles W. Peale
National Park Service

Larry A. Maxwell

Haym Solomon
Alleged Portrait

Robert Morris
By Robert Edge Pine
Between 1784-1788

James Swan
By Gilbert Stuart
1795

Rev. John Gano
Artist & Source Uncredited ca. 1780
Continental Army Chaplain
New York Public Library

Major Gen. Richard Montgomery
By Charles W. Peale
Killed at Battle of Quebec Dec. 1775
Philadelphia Museum

What Did They Wear?

Enoch Crosby
By Samuel Lovett Waldo 1830
Smithsonian

Crispus Attucks
Alleged Portrait 1854
Encyclopedia Britannica

Bernardo de Galvez
By Marino S. Maella
1783

Alexander Hamilton
By John Trumbull
Painted ca. 1792-1797

Tadeusz Kościuszko
By Karl Schweiart
Painted after 1802

Larry A. Maxwell

Gilbert du Motier Marquis de Lafayette
By Joseph-Desire Court
1791

Joan Clerk van der Capellen tot den pol
By Johan A. Kladenbach
1784-1800

Charles Henri Hector Comte d'Estaing
By Jean-Baptiste Le Brun
1769

Nathaniel Greene
By Gilbert Stuart
Nathaniel Greene Homestead

Francis Marion
Engraving by Granger

What Did They Wear?

John Paul Jones Pirate
By A Park ca. 1779
Tabernacle Walk London

John Paul Jones
By Charles W. Peale
ca. 1781

Other Historical Illustrations

The Bloody Massacre
By Paul Revere

Larry A. Maxwell

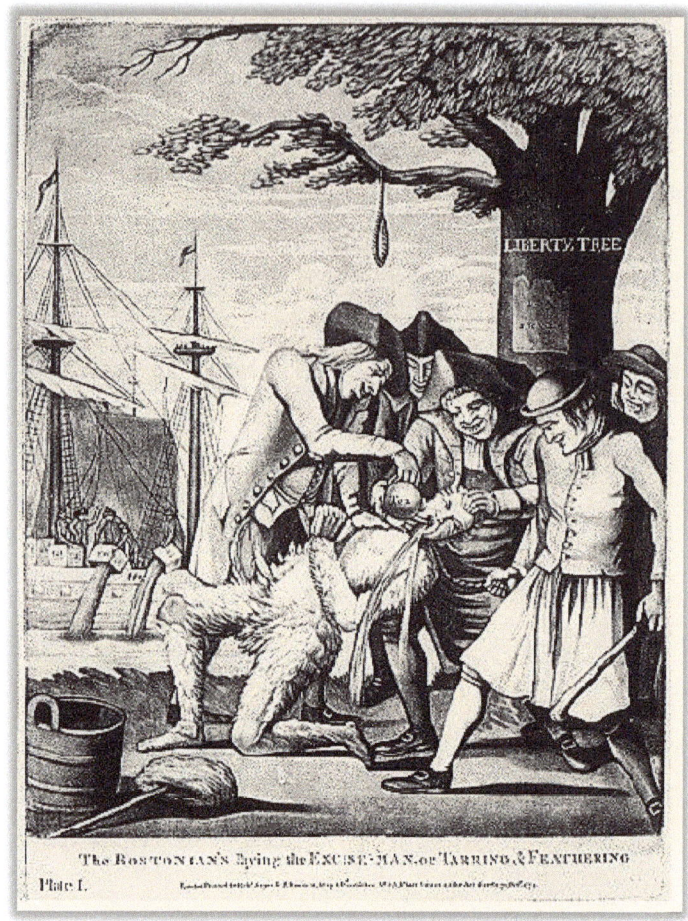

Opposition to the Stamp Act
The Bostonian's Paying the Excise Man
Philip Dawe, London, 1774

The Boston Tea Party
Engraving from 1773
New York Public Library

What Did They Wear?

Peter Salem at Bunker Hill
William C. Nell, 1855

British Prison Ship HMS Jersey
Docked in New York
18th Century Engraving

Larry A. Maxwell

Friedrich Von Germann Drawings from the Revolution

Friedrich Von Germain was a Captain in the Hesse-Kanau Army. He arrived in Canada in 1775. He was present later at the Battle of Saratoga and taken prisoner. He did several sketches of uniforms he saw. These are an incredible source. He shows the facing colors for each regiment. He accurately shows the cut down Regimental Coats and the caps adapted by the Crown Forces during the Burgoyne Campaign and the non-cut-down coats of the Hessians and Jagers.

21st Regiment 1778

62nd Regiment 1778

Artillery 1778

Hessen Hanau Regt. Erbprinz 1778

Braunshew Regt. v. Riedesel 1778

Braunshew Dragoon Regt. 1778

Braunshew Jager 1778

What Did They Wear?

Scottish Soldier

Canadian Soldier

British Soldier 1766

American Soldier

American Officer 1778

Larry A. Maxwell

The Royal Warrant of 1768

This is Very Important for those doing a British Army Impression. You should follow these orders UNLESS you have documentation for doing otherwise.

A Royal Warrant was issued in 1768 which specified what soldiers in an Infantry Unit should wear. The following information is extracted from that warrant.

UNIFORM OF THE OFFICERS

- The number of each regiment to be on the buttons of the uniforms of the Officers and men.
- The coats to be lapelled to the waist with the color of the facing of the regiment, and the color not to be varied from what is particularly specified hereafter.
  They may be without embroidery or lace; but, if the Colonel thinks proper, either gold or silver embroidered or laced buttonholes are permitted.
- To have cross pockets, and sleeves with round cuffs, and no slits. The lapels and cuffs to be of the same breadth as is ordered for the men.

EPAULETTES

- The Officers of grenadiers to wear an epaulette on each shoulder.
- Those of the battalion to wear one on the right shoulder. They are to be either of embroidery or lace, with gold or silver fringe.

WAISTCOATS

- The waistcoats to be plain, without either embroidery or lace.

SWORDS and SWORD KNOTS

- The swords of each regiment to be uniform, and the sword-knots of the whole to be crimson and gold in stripes.
- The hilts of the swords to be either gilt or silver, according to the color of the buttons on the uniforms.

HATS

- The hats to be laced either with gold or silver, as hereafter specified, and to be cocked uniformly.

SASHES AND GORGETS

- The sashes to be of crimson silk and worn round the waist.
- The King's arms to be engraved on the gorgets; also, the number of the regiment.
  They are to be either gilt or silver, according to the color of the buttons on the uniforms.
  The badges of those regiments which are entitled to any, are also to be engraved.

CAPS, FUZILS AND POUCHES
FOR THE GRENADIER OFFICERS

- The Officers of the grenadiers to wear black bear-skin caps; and to have fusils, shoulder-belts, and pouches.
- The shoulder-belts to be white or buff, according to the color of their waistcoats.

ESPONTOONS

- The battalion Officers to have espontoons.

GAITERS

- The whole to have black linen gaiters, with black buttons, small stiff tops, black garters, and uniform buckles.

SEARJEANT'S COATS

- The coats of the Serjeants to be lapelled to the waist, with the color of the facing of the regiment.
- The buttonholes of the coat to be of white braid.
- Those on the waistcoats to be plain.
- The Serjeants of grenadiers to have fusils, pouches, and caps.
- Those of the battalion to have halberds, and no pouches.

SERJEANT'S SASHES

- `The sashes to be of crimson worsted, with a stripe of the color of the facing of the regiment and worn round the waist.
- Those of the regiments which are faced with red, to have a stripe of white.

CORPORAL'S COATS

- The coats of the Corporals to have a silk epaulette on the right shoulder.

GRENADIER'S COATS

- The coats of the grenadiers to have the usual round wings of red cloth on the point of the shoulder, with six loops of the same sort of lace as on the buttonholes, and a border round the bottom.

PRIVATE MEN'S COATS

- The men's coats to be looped with worsted lace, but no border. The ground of the lace to be white, with colored stripes.
- To have white [metal] buttons.
- The breadth of the lace which is to make the loop round the button-hole, to be about half an inch.
- Four loops to be on the sleeves, and four on the pockets, with two on each side of the slit behind.

LAPPELS, SLEEVES AND POCKETS

- The breadth of all the lapels to be three inches, to reach down to the waist, and not to be wider at the top than at the bottom.
- The sleeves of the coats to have a small round cuff, without any slit, and to be made so that they may be unbuttoned and let down.
- The whole to have cross pockets, but no flaps to those of the waistcoat.
- The cuffs of the sleeve which turns up, to be three inches and a half deep.
- The flap on the pocket of the coat to be sewed down, and the pocket to be cut in the lining of the coat.

SHOULDER BELTS AND WAIST BELTS

- The breadth of the shoulder-belts to be two inches and three quarters
- That of the waist belt to be two inches
- Those regiments which have buff waistcoats are to have buff-colored accoutrements.
- Those which have white waistcoats are to have white.

DRUMMER'S AND FIFER'S COATS

- The coats of the drummers and fifers of all the royal regiments are to be red, faced and lapelled with blue, and laced with royal lace.

What Did They Wear?

- The waistcoats, breeches, and lining of the coats, to be of the same color as that which is ordered for their respective regiments.
- The coats of the drummers and fifers of those regiments which are faced with red, are to be white, faced, lapelled, and lined with red; they are to wear red waistcoats and breeches.
- Those of all the other regiments are to be of the color of the facing of their regiments, faced and lapelled with red.
- The waistcoats, breeches, and lining of those which have buff or white coats, are to be red.
- Those of all the others are to be of the same color as that which is ordered for the men.
- To be laced in such manner as the Colonel shall think fit. The lace to be of the color of that on the soldiers' coats.
- The coats have no hanging sleeves behind.

DRUMMER'S AND FIFER'S CAPS

- The drummers and fifers to have black bearskin caps.
- On the front, the King's crest, of silver-plated metal, on a black ground, with trophies of colors and drums.
- The number of the regiment on the back part; as also the badge, if entitled to any, as ordered for the grenadiers.

GRENADIER'S CAPS

- The caps of the grenadiers to be of black bearskin.
  On the front, the King's crest, of silver-plated metal, on a black ground, with the motto, *Nec aspera terrent*.
  A grenade on the back part, with the number of the regiment on it.
- The royal regiments, and the six old corps, are to have the crest and grenade, and also the other particulars as hereafter specified.
  The badge of the royal regiments is to be white, and set near the top of the back part of the cap.
- The height of the cap (without the bearskin, which reaches beyond the top) to be twelve inches.

HATS OF THE WHOLE

- The hats of the Serjeants to be laced with silver.
- Those of the Corporals and private men to have a white tape binding.
- The breadth of the whole to be one inch and a quarter; and no more to be on the back part of the brim, than what is necessary to sew it down.
- To have black cockades.

CAPS FOR THE OFFICERS AND MEN OF THE REGIMENTS OF FUZILEERS

- The regiments of fusiliers to have black bear-skin caps.
- They are to be made in the same manner as those which are ordered for the grenadiers, but not so high; and not to have the grenade on the back part.

SWORDS

- All the Serjeants of the regiment, and the whole grenadier company, to have swords.
- The Corporals and private men of the battalion companies (excepting the regiment of Royal Highlanders) to have no swords.
- All the drummers and fifers to have a short sword with a scimitar blade.

GAITERS

- The Serjeants, Corporals, drummers, fifers, and private men, to have black gaiters of the same sort as is ordered for the Officers, also black garters and uniform buckles.

Helpful Books &Resources

Collector's Illustrated Encyclopedia of the American Revolution - George Neumann

Don Troiani's Soldiers of the American Revolution – Also his other Books and Art

Sketch 76: The American Soldier 1775-1781 - Robert L. Klinger

Osprey Publishing – Books about Soldiers of the Revolution

The Company of Military Historians Journals - Magazine

The Journal of the American Revolution - Magazine

The Brigade of the American Revolution Publications – The Dispatch, Woman's Clothing Guide, Military Music.

Some Good Authors: George Neuman, Todd Braisted, Don Hagist, and Phil Weaver

Larry A. Maxwell

About the Author
Larry A. Maxwell

Larry A. Maxwell is a historian, author, reenactor, and historical tailor. He is the Executive Director of The Living History Guild. He and others in the Living History Guild portray the Continental Soldier, Militia, and both Continental and Royal Artillery. They also do portrayals from other time periods.

He was the Chairman of the Company of Military Historians at West Point and is a member of the Brigade of the American Revolution, The British Brigade, and The Continental Line.

He is the New York State Historian for the Town of Patterson, New York where he also serves as a First Responder with the Patterson Fire Department.

He has served as a historical advisor and costumer for various film projects including: The History Channel, The Travel Channel, and for the New York State Department of Parks and Recreation.

He is an author of numerous books and an award-winning journalist who has received the Associated Press Writing Award.

Some of his books include:
- How to Make a Revolutionary War Regimental Coat
- Sybil Rides the True Story of Sybil Ludington, the Female Paul Revere, the Burning of Danbury and Battle of Ridgefield.
- An Encounter with Sybil Ludington

He has travelled around the world speaking in schools and for numerous events and conferences. He is available for speaking engagements.

For more information you may contact him as follows:
Mail: Larry A. Maxwell, 599 Route 311, Patterson, NY 12563
Phone or Text: 845-241-0035
Text is a Better Method Than Email for Contacts.
Email: LarryMaxwell@cheerful.com

Larry A. Maxwell

What Did They Wear?

Larry A. Maxwell

www.ingramcontent.com/pod-product-compliance
Lightning Source LLC
Chambersburg PA
CBHW041528070526
44586CB00002B/12